Put Beginning Readers on the Right Track with
ALL ABOARD READING™

The All Aboard Reading series is especially designed for beginning readers. Written by noted authors and illustrated in full color, these are books that children really *want* to read—books to excite their imagination, expand their interests, make them laugh, and support their feelings. With fiction and nonfiction stories that are high interest and curriculum-related, All Aboard Reading books offer something for every young reader. And with four different reading levels, the All Aboard Reading series lets you choose which books are most appropriate for your children and their growing abilities.

Picture Readers
Picture Readers have super-simple texts, with many nouns appearing as rebus pictures. At the end of each book are 24 flash cards—on one side is a rebus picture; on the other side is the written-out word.

Station Stop 1
Station Stop 1 books are best for children who have just begun to read. Simple words and big type make these early reading experiences more comfortable. Picture clues help children to figure out the words on the page. Lots of repetition throughout the text helps children to predict the next word or phrase—an essential step in developing word recognition.

Station Stop 2
Station Stop 2 books are written specifically for children who are reading with help. Short sentences make it easier for early readers to understand what they are reading. Simple plots and simple dialogue help children with reading comprehension.

Station Stop 3
Station Stop 3 books are perfect for children who are reading alone. With longer text and harder words, these books appeal to children who have mastered basic reading skills. More complex stories captivate children who are ready for more challenging books.

In addition to All Aboard Reading books, look for All Aboard Math Readers™ (fiction stories that teach math concepts children are learning in school); All Aboard Science Readers™ (nonfiction books that explore the most fascinating science topics in age-appropriate language); All Aboard Poetry Readers™ (funny, rhyming poems for readers of all levels); and All Aboard Mystery Readers™ (puzzling tales where children piece together evidence with the characters).

All Aboard for happy reading!

For Mom and Dad—B.H.

GROSSET & DUNLAP
Published by the Penguin Group
Penguin Group (USA) Inc., 375 Hudson Street, New York, New York 10014, USA
Penguin Group (Canada), 90 Eglinton Avenue East, Suite 700,
Toronto, Ontario M4P 2Y3, Canada
(a division of Pearson Penguin Canada Inc.)
Penguin Books Ltd., 80 Strand, London WC2R 0RL, England
Penguin Group Ireland, 25 St. Stephen's Green, Dublin 2, Ireland
(a division of Penguin Books Ltd.)
Penguin Group (Australia), 250 Camberwell Road, Camberwell, Victoria 3124, Australia
(a division of Pearson Australia Group Pty. Ltd.)
Penguin Books India Pvt. Ltd., 11 Community Centre, Panchsheel Park,
New Delhi—110 017, India
Penguin Group (NZ), 67 Apollo Drive, Rosedale, North Shore 0632, New Zealand
(a division of Pearson New Zealand Ltd.)
Penguin Books (South Africa) (Pty.) Ltd., 24 Sturdee Avenue,
Rosebank, Johannesburg 2196, South Africa

Penguin Books Ltd., Registered Offices:
80 Strand, London WC2R 0RL, England

Photo Credit: Cover: © Warren Faidley/Weatherstock; title page: © AP Photo/Kevork
Djansezian; page 5: © AP Photo/Don Ryan; page 7: © AP Photo/Vincent Laforet;
page 12: © AP Photo/Ray Fairall; page 19: © Sproetniek/istockphoto;
page 23: © AP Photo/Wilfredo Lee; page 24: © AP Photo/Wilfredo Lee;
page 25: © AP Photo/NOAA; page 30: © AP Photo/NOAA; page 36: © Gene Krebs/istockphoto;
page 38: © AP Photo/Nick Ut; page 40: © Kirill Putchenko; page 43: © AP Photo/Bill Haber

Library of Congress Control Number: 2010009737

ISBN 978-0-448-45466-5   10 9 8 7 6 5 4 3 2 1

All Aboard Science Reader™ Station Stop 3

HURRICANES
WEATHERING THE STORM

by Benjamin Hojem
with photographs
illustrations by Stephen Marchesi

Grosset & Dunlap
An Imprint of Penguin Group (USA) Inc.

CHAPTER ONE

A Terrible Storm

On August 29, 2005, Hurricane Katrina swept into the city of New Orleans, Louisiana. Four days earlier, a milder version of the same hurricane hit the southern tip of Florida. After crossing through Florida, the storm found an area of very warm water in the Gulf of Mexico. This warm water caused the small hurricane to grow into a massive hurricane. On August 28, Katrina became a Category 5 hurricane, the highest and most dangerous category of hurricanes. Radar and weather satellites could see that the storm was over 400 miles wide. Scientists knew that the most damage would occur wherever the middle of the storm hit.

In the past, other major hurricanes had

come very close to hitting New Orleans, but they landed away from the city. As Katrina gathered strength in the Gulf, scientists realized it was heading straight for New Orleans. On August 28, the mayor ordered most of the people to evacuate, or leave, New Orleans.

A soldier directs traffic in New Orleans after Hurricane Katrina.

Around one million people evacuated New Orleans, but with only a day's notice, not everyone was able to leave. Over 100,000 people remained in the city. After Katrina made landfall, it flooded nearly 80 percent of the city. After the storm, many neighborhoods were under several feet of water. People had to escape the rising floodwaters by climbing onto their roofs. Rescuers used boats to bring these people to safety.

The storm did great damage to the city. The floodwaters destroyed many homes. The water eventually receded, or drained away, but it left layers of dirt on the buildings. Walls and floors of houses rotted and crumbled. Nearly a million people in the New Orleans area lost electricity in their neighborhoods. Many bridges were broken. Worst of all, around 1,800 people died. Today, there are many homes in New Orleans that are still abandoned.

Hurricane Katrina was a terrible disaster. To understand how it happened, you have to understand what hurricanes are, where they come from, and how they work.

The flooding from Hurricane Katrina

CHAPTER TWO

Hurricanes: Giant Storms

Hurricanes are the largest storms on Earth. Believe it or not, hurricanes can grow to over 50,000 feet in altitude. That's over nine miles high! Typically, hurricanes range from 100 to over 500 miles wide. That's a lot compared to the average thunderstorm, which is only 15 miles wide. Hurricane Katrina was very large at 400 miles wide, but it wasn't the biggest ever recorded. The largest hurricane ever recorded was Typhoon Tip in 1979— *typhoon* is another name for a hurricane. At one point, it reached 1,380 miles wide. That's as big as half of the United States!

Other than their size, what make hurricanes so dangerous are their strong winds. Hurricanes have much stronger

A map showing the size of Typhoon Tip

winds than ordinary storms. In order for
a storm to be called a hurricane, its winds
must be at least 74 miles per hour. That's
as fast as a car driving on the highway! But
hurricanes can also carry winds as high as
200 miles per hour! That's faster than the
top speed of most NASCAR racers!

Scientists use the hurricane's wind speed
to categorize the storm. A hurricane is
rated from one to five. Category 1 is the
weakest and Category 5 is the strongest.
Categories 3, 4, and 5 are considered

"major hurricanes." The chart below shows the wind speeds for each category.

Category 1	74 mph–95 mph
Category 2	96 mph–110 mph
Category 3	111 mph–130 mph
Category 4	131 mph–155 mph
Category 5	156 mph and up

In 1969, two men, Herbert Saffir and Bob Simpson, came up with a way to warn people how strong a hurricane was going to be. Herbert Saffir was a civil engineer. Civil engineers are experts in the strengths of buildings. Bob Simpson was a meteorologist. A meteorologist is a scientist who studies the weather. The two men worked together to create a scale that determined how much damage a hurricane would do. The list of categories is called the Saffir-Simpson Hurricane Scale.

When Hurricane Katrina hit New Orleans, its winds were 125 miles per hour, which made it a Category 3 hurricane. A Category 3 hurricane will snap or pull up trees, tear windows out of tall buildings, and destroy walls in weaker buildings like mobile homes. Categories 4 and 5 are even worse. The Saffir-Simpson Hurricane Scale says that a Category 5 hurricane can even destroy well-built houses. Fortunately, it is rare for a Category 5 hurricane to hit the United States. A Category 5 hurricane starts over the ocean and becomes weaker as it gets closer to land, where the water is shallow and cold.

But that's not to say that a Category 5 hurricane has *never* struck the United

The aftermath of Hurricane Andrew

States. Over the last 100 years, three Category 5 hurricanes have hit the United States: the Labor Day Hurricane of 1935, Hurricane Camille in 1969, and Hurricane Andrew in 1992.

Hurricane Andrew hit the southern tip of Florida on August 24, 1992. At the time, it was the most costly natural disaster in the history of the United States. It was a terrible tragedy: 61 people died, and repairing the damage of Hurricane Andrew cost about $30 billion. But that is still less than half the cost of the damage caused by Hurricane Katrina.

CHAPTER THREE

Where and When Hurricanes Strike

Hurricanes can happen in many parts of the world, but they can only form over an ocean. These big storms are called hurricanes when they are in the northern part of the Atlantic Ocean or the northeastern part of the Pacific Ocean— the two oceans on either side of the United States. In other places, they are either called typhoons or cyclones. Some people believe typhoon comes from the Chinese words "tai fung," which means "great wind." Typhoons occur in the northwestern part of the Pacific Ocean. In the southern half of the world, these storms are called cyclones. Cyclones are pulled toward the South Pole, and hurricanes are pulled toward the North Pole. Cyclones will never move

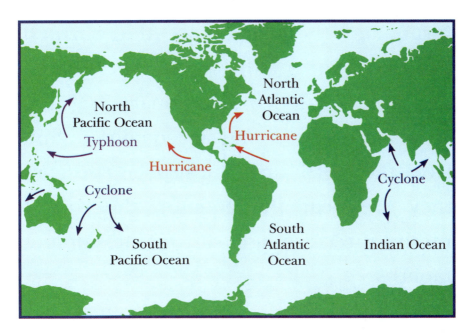

Different names for tropical cyclones in different parts of the world

north to become hurricanes and hurricanes will never move south to become cyclones. Cyclones, hurricanes, and typhoons are really all the same kind of storm, just in different parts of the world.

The scientific name for these storms (regardless of where they are in the world) is *tropical cyclone*. Hurricanes are tropical because they are born in the tropics. Hurricanes need lots of warm water to form, and the tropics are the warmest places on Earth. The tropics are located near the equator, the imaginary line that circles the globe and is equally distant from the North and South poles. Because they are near the equator, the tropics receive direct sunlight during the summer months.

Hurricanes are cyclones because they spin, or cycle, around a point in the center of the storm. In the Northern Hemisphere (the half of the earth which is north of the equator), hurricanes swirl in a counterclockwise direction. In the Southern Hemisphere, they swirl the opposite way. This is called the Coriolis effect and is caused by the earth's rotation. On the equator, there is no Coriolis effect. Even though the water temperatures are hot near the equator, a storm usually needs

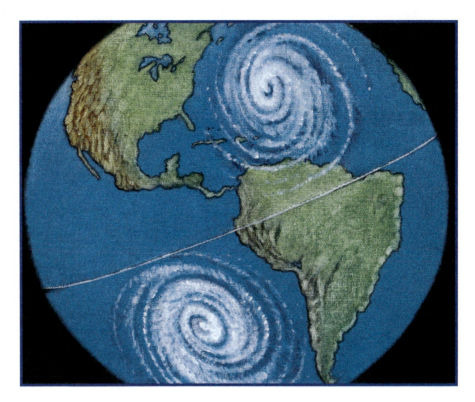

The Coriolis effect

to be at least 300 miles north or south of the equator to become a hurricane.

In order for a tropical cyclone to form, the ocean temperature must be at least 81° Fahrenheit. This is why hurricanes usually form only during the late summer and early fall. At other times, the water is too cold. The official hurricane season for the

United States is from June 1 to November 30. Its peak is August through October.

Most hurricanes that hit the United States come from the Atlantic Ocean. It's very rare for a hurricane to hit the states on the Pacific coast because the water in that part of the Pacific Ocean is usually cooler than 81° Fahrenheit. The last hurricane to hit the United States from the Pacific Ocean was over 150 years ago! It hit San Diego, California, on October 2, 1858. At that time, California had only been a state for eight years. That storm is still the only hurricane to hit California in its entire history!

CHAPTER FOUR

How to Predict the Weather

On average, six hurricanes develop over the Atlantic Ocean every summer. Not all of these hurricanes will hit populated areas, but scientists monitor them just in case. One of the many tools scientists use to monitor a hurricane is a barometer.

A barometer

The barometer was invented in 1643, and it was the very first instrument that could be used to predict the weather. Meteorologists use barometers to measure the pressure in the air. If the barometer shows that the air pressure is falling, it means that a storm is approaching.

Just like other storms, the air pressure falls before a hurricane arrives. Scientists can use barometers to predict the path of a hurricane by looking for the places where the air pressure is falling the most. Wherever the air pressure is the lowest, that is where the hurricane will go next. Unfortunately, the air pressure only drops right in front of the approaching storm. Because of this, barometers can only tell that a storm is approaching roughly six hours before it makes landfall.

CHAPTER FIVE

The Mighty Hurricane Hunters

In order to find out how powerful a hurricane is, meteorologists need to be able to measure the pressure in its center. The inside of a hurricane is a very dangerous place to be, but in the 1940s, meteorologists found a way to safely get inside the storm.

In 1943 an airplane was flown intentionally into a hurricane for the first time. That year, which was in the middle of World War II, British pilots were being trained near Bryan, Texas, when a hurricane was spotted off the coast. Many of the American pilots were afraid to fly their AT-6 airplanes with the storm approaching. This made the British pilots say the airplanes must be poorly built! To prove they were safe, American Colonel

Joe Duckworth successfully flew his AT-6 into the center of the hurricane—*twice*! After the war, because they knew it was safe, the United States Air Force began flying missions into hurricanes in order to study them. This is something that still goes on today. The pilots who fly these missions are called hurricane hunters. They are members of the Air Force Reserve, and always fly the Lockheed-Martin WC-130J. Hurricane hunters fly directly through the center of a hurricane to measure its strongest winds and the pressure at the center of the storm. Their missions usually take around 11 hours to complete.

In a major hurricane, it's dangerous for the hurricane hunters to fly into the hurricane anywhere under 10,000 feet above sea level because the wind is strongest near the ocean. Instead, they fly into the hurricane's center at a safe height and drop an instrument called a dropsonde (say: DROP-sond) that measures the wind speed and air pressure at different heights as it falls. A dropsonde looks like a tube with a parachute on it. It sends its measurements back to the airplane using radio waves.

A dropsonde before it is dropped from a plane

In 1998, the first plane flown without a pilot, called an Aerosonde (say: air-OH-sond), was used to measure a hurricane's winds off the coast of Australia.

A pilot poses with an Aerosonde.

An Aerosonde can fly through a hurricane at 1,000 feet, so it doesn't need dropsondes to take measurements. Someday, these remote-controlled planes might replace the hurricane hunters.

The airplane isn't the only important

tool in studying hurricanes. Before a plane can be sent to take measurements in a hurricane, the hurricanes need to be located. Radar allows the meteorologists to see hurricanes, or storms that may become hurricanes, anywhere in the world.

During World War II, radar was first used to locate airplanes in the sky. Radar finds objects by sending out radio waves in all directions. Some of these radio waves

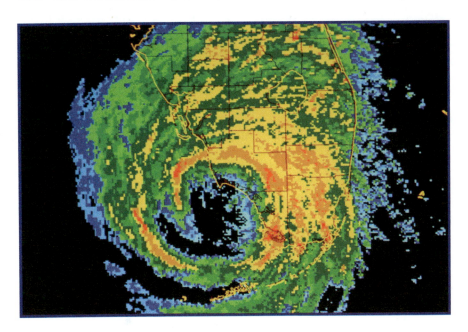

A typical image produced by radar

hit objects and bounce back to the radar station. It was soon discovered that radar could also detect rain in the sky. In the late 1950s, the National Weather Service began using radar to detect hurricanes off the coasts of the United States. Now radar is so sensitive that it can use radio waves to detect and estimate the amounts of rain or wind inside a storm.

Weather satellites are also used to track hurricanes. In 1959, the first weather satellite, the Vanguard 2, was sent into space to track storms. Weather satellites use infrared radiation to see developing weather.

These technologies, which allow us to find and take measurements of the conditions inside and around hurricanes, have taught us how and why hurricanes happen.

Chapter Six

The Brief and Wondrous Life of a Hurricane

Now that scientists can track storms all over the world, they know how hurricanes develop and where they come from.

Most hurricanes that reach the United States start on the other side of the Atlantic Ocean. They usually begin as smaller storms off the coast of northwest Africa. Hot, dry air from Africa's Sahara Desert mixes with the cooler, more moist air from the Sahel, a region of grasslands south of the Sahara. When the air from the Sahara and the air from the Sahel meet, they try to mix.

Sometimes the mixing of the air from the Sahara and the Sahel will create a low pressure system. The air from Africa is warm, so it rises very quickly—leaving a

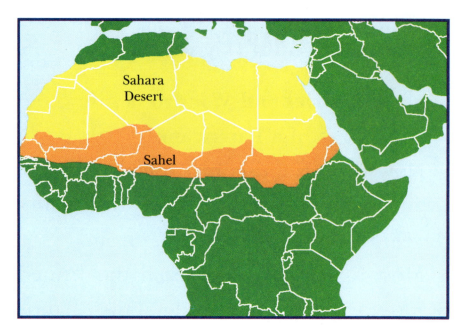

A map of the Sahara Desert

space with very little air that wants to be filled. This low pressure space pulls in a lot of moist air once it moves over the Atlantic Ocean. This is when it starts to grow into a major storm.

If the pressure is really low, then too much air tries to push its way into the storm's center at one time. Not all of it can get in, but so much air is pushing to get into the center that the air can't stop moving. The Coriolis effect helps this air move together in one direction around the center of the storm.

The crowd of air spinning around the center of the storm makes it even more difficult for the outside air to reach the center. The air in the middle is still being warmed by the warm ocean beneath it, so it keeps rising. Without new air coming in to replace it, the pressure becomes lower, which makes it pull even harder. The outside air spins faster and faster, and the storm gets bigger and bigger.

This process is what gives a hurricane's eye its conical, or conelike, shape. The eye is the name for the center of the storm. Inside the eye, the air is very warm and can be very calm. In fact, if you were standing in the eye, you would see blue sky or the stars above you. The eye of a storm can be as small as five miles wide or as large as 200 miles—that would be more than a two-hour drive! Most hurricanes have eyes that are about 20 to 40 miles across.

The strongest winds surround the eye of the storm. The fast-moving air around the eye creates the eyewall. Sometimes a hurricane will develop a larger eyewall around the original eyewall. When this happens, the inner eyewall weakens and

An aerial view of the eye of a hurricane

collapses. This can weaken a hurricane for a brief time. Before Hurricane Katrina hit New Orleans, it was a Category 5 hurricane with 175 mph winds. It became a Category 3 storm before landfall when it replaced its original eyewall with a new eyewall. This made it a weaker storm, but also a much larger storm.

There are two ways a hurricane can die. Water and heat are necessary to maintain the low pressure in a hurricane's eye, so a hurricane will weaken rapidly if it hits land. Also, if the hurricane moves too far north in the ocean, it will weaken because the water there is too cold. As the pressure rises, the hurricane's center stops pulling on the outside air. The spinning eyewall collapses, the storm stops spinning, and the hurricane turns into a regular thunderstorm.

CHAPTER SEVEN

What's in a Name?

To help identify and keep track of hurricanes, meteorologists give them names. This is something that has been done all over the world for a long time.

The Spanish were probably the first people to give names to hurricanes. After Christopher Columbus landed in the West Indies in 1492, he and the Spanish settlers who followed him encountered hurricanes. The Spanish were Catholic, and in Catholic tradition, each day of the year has its own saint. So when a hurricane hit, the Spanish settlers would name it after the saint of that particular day.

But outside of the West Indies, no one named hurricanes. That is, until over a hundred years ago, when an Australian meteorologist named Clement Wragge began naming hurricanes after people, including politicians, he didn't like! In 1953, American meteorologists started giving hurricanes names, too, but only to tell them apart. Now there are six different lists of hurricane names that scientists choose from. The lists have one name for each letter of the alphabet, except for the letters Q, U, X, Y, and Z. One list is used per year and the storms are given names in alphabetical order. After a major hurricane, its name is retired forever, and replaced with a new name. But the new name must start with the same letter as the old name. Both Katrina and Andrew have been retired from the lists, which means that no future hurricane can have those names.

Here's a list of retired hurricane names and the year in which they were retired:

Agnes, 1972	David, 1979
Alicia, 1983	Dean, 2007
Allen, 1980	Hazel, 1954
Allison, 2001	Hilda, 1964
Andrew, 1992	Hortense, 1996
Anita, 1977	Dennis, 2005
Audrey, 1957	Diana, 1990
Betsy, 1965	Diane, 1955
Beulah, 1967	Donna, 1960
Bob, 1991	Dora, 1964
Camille, 1969	Edna, 1968
Carla, 1961	Elena, 1985
Carmen, 1974	Eloise, 1975
Carol, 1954	Fabian, 2003
Celia, 1970	Felix, 2007
Cesar, 1996	Fifi, 1974
Charley, 2004	Flora, 1963
Cleo, 1964	Floyd, 1999
Connie, 1955	Fran, 1996

Frances, 2004	**Janet**, 1955
Frederic, 1979	**Jeanne**, 2004
Georges, 1998	**Joan**, 1988
Gilbert, 1988	**Juan**, 2003
Gloria, 1985	**Katrina**, 2005
Gustav, 2008	**Lili**, 2002
Hattie, 1961	**Luis**, 1995
Keith, 2000	**Marilyn**, 1995
Klaus, 1990	**Michelle**, 2001
Lenny, 1999	**Mitch**, 1998
Hugo, 1989	**Noel**, 2007
Ike, 2008	**Opal**, 1995
Inez, 1966	**Paloma**, 2008
Ione, 1955	**Rita**, 2005
Iris, 2001	**Roxanne**, 1995
Isabel, 2003	**Stan**, 2005
Isidore, 2002	**Wilma**, 2005
Ivan, 2004	

CHAPTER EIGHT

Water, Water Everywhere

What makes hurricanes so destructive? Even though a hurricane's strength is measured by its winds, the flooding it causes to cities close to the ocean is much more destructive. This is especially true in a place like New Orleans, which is surrounded by water. But rain from a hurricane's clouds is not what causes major

A typical street scene after a hurricane

flooding. What does? It is the water from the ocean beneath the storm.

A hurricane always spins in the same direction, and this spinning pushes the ocean water into a single massive wave that travels with the hurricane. This giant wave is called a storm surge. The storm surge created by a major hurricane can be over 20 feet above sea level, the natural height of the ocean's water. When the hurricane hits land, this storm surge is often higher than the coastal land. Many houses in coastal towns where there are frequent hurricanes are built on stilts to protect them from storm surges.

But coastal towns haven't always been prepared for the destruction of a major hurricane. The deadliest hurricane in the history of the United States hit Galveston, Texas, in 1900. It was a Category 4

Waves from a hurricane pound the shore.

hurricane, and it killed between 6,000 and 12,000 people. Galveston is located on an island in the Gulf of Mexico. The highest point on the island was less than 9 feet above sea level and the hurricane's storm surge is believed to have been around 15 feet high. Only the most solidly built homes survived the storm. Even though a hurricane's destructiveness is measured by the strength of its wind, a storm surge is much more destructive to low-lying coastal towns and cities.

Chapter Nine

It's a Twister!

Coastal areas like New Orleans usually receive the full force of a hurricane's destructive power, but once a hurricane travels inland, it can still be deadly. A hurricane weakens and often dies when it travels over land, but once it hits land, it can also produce tornadoes. In fact, more than half of all hurricanes that reach land in the United States will produce at least one tornado. This is because the strong winds from the hurricane mix with the weaker winds below it. This mixing of strong winds with weak winds is what produces a tornado. Hurricane Ivan in 2004 holds the record for most tornadoes spawned in the US: 17 in just three days!

What exactly is a tornado? A tornado is a

Twisters produced by a hurricane

spinning mass of air that looks like a funnel. The widest part of the funnel reaches all the way up to the storm's clouds, and the point of the funnel touches down to the ground. Small tornadoes can be hundreds of feet wide and big tornadoes can measure up to a mile wide! They usually last for only a few minutes at a time, but their winds can sometimes be even stronger than the most powerful hurricanes' winds.

Chapter Ten

The Flooding of New Orleans

A tornado can be dangerous, but that is not what damaged the city of New Orleans. New Orleans is close to the water, which makes it the perfect place for a hurricane to strike. Unlike other places in Louisiana, New Orleans is not located directly on the Gulf of Mexico, the large body of water just south of the United States. But New Orleans is still vulnerable to storm surges. That's because it is located in an area called the Mississippi River Delta. This is where the Mississippi River meets the Gulf of Mexico. The land here isn't much higher than sea level. In fact, in New Orleans, almost half of the land is below sea level. There is nothing to protect the city from a powerful storm surge.

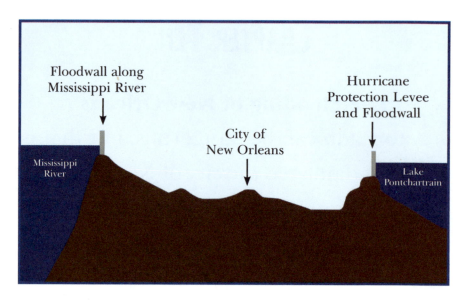

Levees protect New Orleans from flooding.

Hurricane Katrina's storm surge came up from the Atlantic Ocean through Lake Pontchartrain. The lake is on the north shore of the city and is connected to the Gulf of Mexico. In the past, people built walls around the city to keep the water out. These walls are called levees (say: LEV-ees). The levees were 23 feet tall on the Mississippi River and 17.5 feet tall on Lake Pontchartrain. They were built out of clay, steel, and concrete, which made them strong, but not indestructible. The engineers knew that if a powerful hurricane caused the water to rise high enough, the levees might let water in, or even break completely. Katrina's storm surge was around 18 feet high when it reached New Orleans. New Orleans's levees had survived weaker hurricanes with smaller storm surges, but were overpowered by this mighty storm. The levees broke in

A closeup view of a New Orleans levee

several places and the water from the rain and the storm surge flooded the city.

Today, New Orleans is still recovering from the devastation of Katrina. Many people who moved away after the storm have returned, and engineers are working to rebuild the levees to withstand another storm like Katrina. In the future, New Orleans will be better prepared for a major hurricane, but hurricanes will still be a major problem for the city and other coastal towns and cities like it.

CHAPTER ELEVEN

Hurricanes Past and Hurricanes Future

Most hurricanes die in just over a week without doing any damage, but recent destructive hurricanes like Katrina have caused a lot of people to worry about the potential for more deadly hurricanes in the future. Most scientists agree that the earth has been getting warmer over the past few decades. This is called global warming. Since hurricanes are fueled by heat, some scientists predict that if the earth continues to get warmer, there will be more hurricanes, and these hurricanes will be even stronger than ones in the past.

The earth's temperature has changed many times over its 4.5 billion–year history. Some scientists think that a warming of the earth's oceans may have caused the

extinction of the dinosaurs. According to their theory, a large asteroid that landed in the ocean 65 million years ago heated the ocean to over 120° Fahrenheit. This allowed giant hurricanes to form that spewed water vapor into the earth's atmosphere. This blocked out sunlight and cooled the planet to a point where most of the plant and animal life became extinct.

Other scientists are investigating the

possibility that a warmer Earth has recently impacted the frequency of hurricanes. Their evidence says that between 1,000 and 3,000 years ago, hurricanes hit the Gulf Coast three to five times more frequently than they do today. These scientists think that these hurricanes may have had a large impact on the Mayan Indians, who at the time lived in what is now Mexico and Central America. One of their most powerful gods was Hurakan, the god of wind and storms. This is where the word hurricane comes from.

Not long after the end of the Mayan civilization, the world experienced a period of cooling called the Little Ice Age. The earth may have begun cooling as early as the 12th century, and these cooler temperatures lasted until around 1850. Since then, the earth has been warming up. Scientists who study global warming think that humans may be responsible for this. The pollution created by factories, cars, and the animals raised for food could be trapping heat in the atmosphere and causing this rise in temperature.

It's possible that if global temperatures continue to rise, more powerful hurricanes will be seen. If this happens, these storms could have as much of an impact on our civilization as they had on civilizations of the past.